Journal to Gratitude

Edited by

DAVID O'BRIEN

A Collection of
Prayers, Poems & Reflections

Organized Around The

Spiritual Exercises of Saint Ignatius
(1491 – 1556)

Table Of Contents

General Acknowledgements & Donations:

Journal to Gratitude includes spiritual journaling by many authors over thousands of years. For the vast majority of these authors, their material reward rarely exceeded a meal or a place to sleep. Their words were a labor of love; an expression of gratitude. They gave back what had been given to them.

In keeping with this labor of love, my poetic partner, Martha Conway, and I are donating the proceeds of this book to two Jesuit affiliated organizations that promote spiritual outreach and journaling. After printing and distribution costs, all proceeds will be divided amongst two non-profit organizations: 1) Ignatian Associates, http://www.ignatianassociates.org/ and 2) Cristo Rey Jesuit High School, http://www.cristoreytc.org/

Personal Acknowledgements

Many people have helped in the development of *Journal to Gratitude*. The collection could not have happened without the constant motivation of friends who kept encouraging. It would have been easy to quit were it not for those who kept asking the "are we there yet" type of questions and offering positive feedback. Several friends offered critiques that resulted in changes when *Journal to Gratitude* needed more work.

For editorial feedback and constant motivation: Mary Beth O'Brien, Devin O'Brien, Judy Wolff, Roy Wolff, Mary Satterstrom, Denise D'Aurora and Mike Flynn. For spiritual companionship and guidance along the way:Martha Conway, Wayne Hergot, Delores Olson, Chris Manahan S.J., Thomas Cinadr, Connie Pelner, Joseph Claus, Bishop Paul Dudley, Larry Gillick S.J., Michael Harter S.J., and Fr. Kevin Finnegan.

Last, but not least, a general thank you to the Society of Jesus and their 450 plus years of service. This publication would not have been possible without their legacy of leadership in spiritual outreach. The Wisconsin Province of the Society of Jesus deserves a special thank you for their ongoing assistance with the Ignatian Associates.

† Introduction
....

In its simplest form, *Journal to Gratitude* is a collection of scripture and poetic prayer organized around the *Spiritual Exercises* of Saint Ignatius. The scriptures are popular readings recommended to those going through the exercises. The poetic prayer selections were either written by Martha Conway and I or they were selected from the writings of others for their relevance to the *Spiritual Exercises.*

The *Spiritual Exercises* are more than casual prayer. The exercises, as originally designed by Saint Ignatius, are done over a 30 day period that helps a retreatant discern their relationship with God. Although most commonly known as a set of mediations and contemplations for people about to enter the Catholic Order of Jesuits (Society of Jesus), they are currently done by more laity than pre-ordained people around the globe. The exercises are performed by people of all faiths. Like any other use of the word "exercise", the *Spiritual Exercises* require effort and concentration. Seeing God in our life generally requires a new ability and we have to work, even push ourselves, to achieve and maintain this vision.

In a more expansive form, *Journal to Gratitude* is a reflection on how journaling has been an integral part of spiritual journeys throughout time. There are many forms of prayer and relating to God available to us. Of all the forms to express our relationship with God, journaling seemed as appropriate for me as it probably did for the early authors. The early biblical authors used a form of journaling to record their spiritual journey. Excellent prose was not their greatest strength. Being inspired by the Holy Spirit was their gift. You are invited to partake in this tradition.

Martha Conway and I did our initial *Spiritual Exercises* as part of a formation program for the lay group known as the Ignatian Associates. Information on the Ignatian Associates is provided in the last chapter of this book. Although we did our exercises at different times, our prayer forms embraced poetic reflections and journaling from the start. The journaling done by the earliest biblical authors, some 3,500 years ago, was an outgrowth of their effort to communicate with the God in their lives. Like *Journal to Gratitude*, poetic reflections were a significant part of their spirituality. Of the most commonly recognized 66 books in the Christian bible, the poetic Psalms are the largest.

One of the beauties of writing down our humble efforts to communicate with God is that we can, and do, go back to them. Somehow, those moments of intense prayer and Godly communication come back as we, and hopefully you, re-read those words. *Journal to Gratitude* encapsulates our effort, our journey, toward a gratitude for God in our lives. By sharing our journaling to gratitude, we invite you to begin or continue your own spiritual journal.

† Journaling and Spirituality

Prior to writing *Journal to Gratitude* and doing the *Spiritual Exercises*, I never really knew how to respond to someone who talked about having a personal relationship with God. Because I had not experienced their kind of personal relationship with God, I couldn't relate to what they were saying. To make my response even harder, some of those conversations were with non-Catholics who had a better command of the bible and freely spoke about God in their lives. In fact, in a few situations, those conversations were with non-Christians. Having grown up Catholic and graduating from a Jesuit University, I felt equipped with knowledgeable facts. However, there was something about the personal relationship question I didn't quite get.

Knowing that the earliest Christian authors were writing almost 3,500 years ago, I realized that the personal relationship with God question went back to the beginning of time. I came to wonder what enabled these early spiritual journalists. Most probably, I was more formally educated than them. With two master's degrees and undergraduate minors in Philosophy and Theology, it was very likely that I possessed more knowledgeable facts than most of the early biblical authors. Yet, I was not able to respond affirmatively about having a personal relationship with God. Not only did these early biblical authors lack advanced degrees in theology, they were shepherds, farmers, tent-makers, physicians, fishermen, priests, philosophers and kings. Something was different and, while knowledge is good, knowledge was certainly not the differentiator. Oddly enough, my factual knowledge tendencies led to an interesting awareness.

While studying individual biblical authors certainly had merit, the answer to a personal relationship with God lied in the fact that there were so many people throughout history who obviously had such personal relationships. Rather than studying the facts of one author's spiritual journey, there was much to learn by the variety and magnitude of spiritual journaling throughout history. Facts like there being approximately 50 versions of the Christian bible in existence today and that it has been translated into 2,000 languages highlighted the importance of spiritual journaling in seeking a personal relationship with God. The Christian Bible has sold more than any other publication in western civilization.

Some of the people who helped edit *Journal to Gratitude* suggested that the scripture be limited to the chapter and verse identifiers. Hence, everyone might look up their own preferred version. It really comes down to personal choice and no one choice works for everyone. In light of the number of bible versions, I decided to use major verse texts from the New American Bible and insert other favorite readings (chapter and verse) for supplemental scripture reading.

The gospel authors wrote many years after the events and many did not personally know Jesus. For instance, John's gospel was written around AD 90; Luke's gospels are estimated to have been written between AD 80 and 90; Matthew and Mark were written around AD 70. Last but not least, Paul not only came after Jesus, but he persecuted Christians.

The church recognizes the time differences between the gospel events and when they were written. The church's explanation of this time difference is that the authors were inspired by the Holy Spirit. The church does not infer that God dictated the gospels word for word to the authors. The Holy Spirit guided these people to record what God wanted them to communicate. Prior to the Holy Spirit empowering them to write, they had to develop their spirituality and writing ability. It did not come to them in an instant. They could not succeed in their task by simply taking a creative writing class. They had to develop their spirituality and they must have started by journaling what they believed the Holy Spirit was saying to them. Just as the Holy Spirit was available to these authors, the Holy Spirit is available to all of us today. God did not just come to us during creation or while Jesus was physically on earth. The Garden of Eden is still here and so is the Holy Spirit. Both invite us today as much as they did in the past.

Words and Spirituality

Before reading the verse and poetic selections, please pause and reflect on the importance of words, written words, in all of our spirituality. If you are a scholar of biblical verse, an accomplished poet, or a novice to spiritual journaling, you need words. Once written, our words can be revisited by ourselves and others. The importance of our individual spiritual expression should not be measured by our scholarly writing ability. When it comes to spirituality and words, we all have equal access to God. God does not care what you did or wrote yesterday. God cares about where your heart and soul are at this moment.

In the first chapter of the Gospel of John, he captures the role of words in our spirituality.

In the beginning was the Word,

and the Word was with God,

and the Word was God.

He was in the beginning with God.

All things came to be through him

and without him nothing came to be

what came to be through him was life

and this life was the life of the human race;

the light shines in the darkness,

and the darkness has not overcome it

…And the Word was made flesh and

Made his dwelling among us…

In the 1 John 1, he continues this message..

The Word of Life

What was from the beginning, what we have heard,

what we have seen with our eyes,

what we looked upon and touched with our hands concerns the Word of life

for the life was made visible

we have seen it and testify to it

and proclaim to you the eternal life

that was with the Father and made visible to us what we have seen and heard

we proclaim now to you

so that you too may have fellowship with us;

for our fellowship is with the Father and with his Son, Jesus Christ

We are writing this so that our joy may be complete.

John's suggestion is clearly about communicating with the God transformed into flesh. In John's case and ours, one of the best methods of communicating with someone is to write it down. No one knows what we think. While people can clearly hear what we say and we should pray with words, I believe writing is superior. If John had only talked to God, only those who were there would have heard it. Now, because it was written, all of us can share in John's spiritual journey. With written communication, we can carefully choose words. Often, much time is spent condensing feelings and words into powerful poetic expressions.

There are numerous reasons to write as we experience God, but my favorite is exemplified from the perspective of a parent. As a father, I have a wooden box filled with love notes from people I care about. I have been blessed with many that appreciated my humble human efforts. Without putting my children above other relationships, but to make the point about the power of a parent receiving a love note, I would like to summarize how God might feel getting a love note from one of us.

Creating and nurturing my children has been at the essence of my being. Whenever they went off to camp on their own and sent love letters home, they affirmed me and I put those letters in my wooden box. Their love and appreciation not only warmed my heart, it affirmed me. In a unique way, they give me back life like I gave them life. They affirm that the choices I made along the way, for them, were the right ones.

And so I believe it is with God. Having been made in his image and likeness, writing down what we feel about our relationship with God affirms his creation. As the biblical saying goes, "seek and you will find; ask and you will receive". When I seek and ask for God, I receive God's presence in my life. I imagine that, just like I feel joy when a child of mine expresses love for me, so God must feel appreciated and want to communicate more with me. And so my spirituality, my relationship with God, my journey to gratitude grows.

Saint Ignatius' Journey to Gratitude

There are many life stories that could be used to explain a journey to gratitude. One of the greatest things about Ignatius of Loyola (eventually Saint Ignatius) is that he is a perfect case study in examining spiritual versus non-spiritual life choice tensions. Ignatius spent almost half of his life silencing his spirituality. The story of a lay person journeying away from a life of minimal, to actualized, spirituality is the story of Ignatius. Almost 15 years passed between his initial spiritual awakening and eventual ordination. During his time of transformation, Ignatius continually changed the norm of his yesterday lay behavior.

Ignatius' journey from a vain personal and worldly life to an actualized spiritual life contains lessons that are as meaningful today as they were in the 1500's.

In 1491, Ignatius of Loyola was born into a noble Basque Spanish family. For 65 years, he lived in a society that was enjoying global influence and power. As noted by Christopher Columbus's discovery of America in 1492, Spain was at the center of a rapidly expanding world. Spain's influence and power were at a peak. Life was good for many, especially those who enjoyed privilege.

As a young nobleman, Ignatius enjoyed privilege. He did an excellent job of fitting in with the less than spiritual culture of the times. At the age of sixteen, Ignatius was given a job as a page in the court. From this time until age thirty when he was a soldier, his actions were anything but saintly. His behavior norms during this time included the lavish court culture, enjoying the ladies, gambling, interpersonal swordplay/fighting and formal soldiering on the battlefield. In his autobiography "The Pilgrims Testament", this young Ignatius is described as "a man given to the follies of the world; and what he enjoyed most was exercise with arms, having a great and foolish desire to win fame."

Eventually, Ignatius' spiritual journey would have him break away from old non-spiritual peers. No doubt, his peers did not expect or particularly want to see a spiritual Ignatius emerge. They, and Ignatius himself, probably thought that he was too vain, too sinful, too unworthy to change. Over time, his life became committed to Christ. His new life eventually saw God in all things. Ultimately, he found new peers. How many of us feel that we have had pasts that were too vain, too sinful, or too unworthy to consider changing? In God's eyes, none of us are too unworthy.

Was there a single event that triggered Ignatius' conversion?

Conversions can be associated with any number of events. Like many people, Ignatius' conversion started when he experienced mortality. His world of not needing God began to change when a French cannon ball smashed his legs. With one leg seriously wounded and the other broken, Ignatius began a lengthy period of convalescence. It was during this convalescence that Ignatius started to look for and listen to God. His world of courtly pleasures and excesses ceased to exist. More began to appear as less. Ignatius was vulnerable now. He needed others and, most of all, he needed God.

Pain, either physical, emotional or spiritual, is often part of the conversion mystery. The initial human response is often one of "Why Me". Ignatius' or our "Why Me" could be associated with the loss of a leg, an eye, a stroke, cancer, a job, a spouse, a child, or anything that threatens us. Like Ignatius, we have to choose between becoming bitter or better. Given time and God's grace, we have the opportunity to try and become better.

Was there any purpose in Ignatius' pain?

Ignatius' pain was a small glimpse of the pain that exists in the world. Similarly, many of our own North American concerns about pain are small when compared with the rest of the world. Regardless of the amount or duration of an individual's pain, all pain offers the opportunity to see new creation. While the ultimate imagery of new creation is found in the Pascal Mystery, pain and re-creation experiences do not require the ultimate re-creation of life after death. Ignatius' message to us of seeing God in all things includes looking for God in ourselves and others as we deal with pain.

Ignatius' spiritual journey or pilgrimage spans many years. As Ignatius, the no longer courtly nobleman, not yet ordained priest, and now "common man" struggled with his pain, he wrote the *Spiritual Exercises*. The fact that Ignatius used the word "exercises" in the title is no mistake. The *Spiritual Exercises* are to spiritual growth what the best coaching book is to any sport. Like any great coaching book, the *Spiritual Exercises* lay out a program for you to follow. The participant is called upon to seriously exercise their spirituality. Your current spirituality is not assumed to be the end desired state. You will grow and improve your spirituality. Even after reaching some peak state, ongoing exercise is required to maintain what was achieved.

A Daily Attitude of Gratitude

Several months before I started the *Spiritual Exercises*, I casually asked veterans of the exercises what they were like. How did the exercises impact you personally? My questions were not a formal survey involving large numbers of participants. The more I asked others about the impact of the *Spiritual Exercises* on their lives, the more impressed I was by their heartfelt responses.

Gratitude was the frequent response. Gratitude was expressed for a long list of gifts people experienced. Gratefulness for the Jesuits who generously shared their gifts as we went through the *Spiritual Exercises*; for 500 years of Jesuit tradition; for Saint Ignatius of Loyola and his very human journey; for the lay people who have taken up the roles of mentoring others in spiritual growth.

Many of the respondents noted that they too had preconceived notions about the exercises. They were seasoned adults with years of "spirituality". Some had assumed that their major moments of conversion and spiritual growth were behind them, as well. Many thought they were entering something that would add to their wealth of knowledge.

As these people journeyed through the exercises and many preconceived notions changed, most ventured to describe a larger, and perhaps more difficult to describe, sense of gratefulness that blossomed. These descriptions attempted to put humble words around a new found appreciation for life. They expressed an attitude of gratitude that does not happen every hour but is sincerely felt many days.

Specific life-based grateful examples were as varied as the individuals responding. People spoke about how the *Exercises* helped them to deal with life challenges. While the normal human responses of fear and anxiety did not disappear, their responses were different. Instead of responses that might have previously included an angry "why" response, their responses embodied an attitude of "why not". Aren't our life changes and interruptions inevitable? What appeared different was the awareness that these moments of change, these moments we want to, but cannot, control are our opportunities to see Christ in one another and to be Christ to one another.

At a general level, the grateful responses included personal and quiet descriptions of somewhat mystical moments. Maybe these mystical moments, and they were always expressed as moments versus a continuum, were the result of intense prayer and reflection. My guess is that they were the direct result of simply asking to be able to see God in our daily life. As attitudes changed and eyes began to see God in more things, life choices began to change. If we can, only for a few moments, see God in ourselves, then we can see the God that lives in our neighbor. If we see God in our neighbor, we can see God in all our earthly neighbors. In the end, the general grateful examples simply inferred that our choosing was transformed.

There was a beauty in the responses that I heard. Although retreat exercises usually have a very sober side, and the *Spiritual Exercises* have that as well, I was pleasantly surprised by the sense of beauty I was listening to. Ignatius encourages people to maintain this sense of beauty, this grateful attitude by performing the Examen on a daily basis. The Examen, not to be confused with an examination of conscience, is a daily prayerful exercise where one looks for the existence of God in all of our thoughts, feelings and experiences.

Beyond the poetic reflections on the *Spiritual Exercises*, this introduction would be incomplete if it did not remind the reader of the intended outcome from the *Spiritual Exercises*. Although prayer and adoration are important ingredients of the exercises, the goal is not simply one of prayer and adoration. The goal of the *Exercises* and Ignatian Spirituality is to apply and give back to others what has been gifted to us. Often this new emphasis results in a permanent change to our choosing. I am overwhelmed by the intentions of people to try and see Christ in their neighbors, to live humbly, to accept all things, and lastly, to move beyond these appreciative contemplations and be of service to their neighbors.

There are numerous faith-filled activities and exercises available to Christians. The *Spiritual Exercises* of Saint Ignatius are certainly not the only path to an enhanced spirituality. However, from a personal and perhaps biased perspective, the *Spiritual Exercises* of Saint Ignatius "win the prize" of beautifully helping us realize that all of us are made in the image and likeness of God. While this book aims to capture the sense of beauty that comes from doing the *Spiritual Exercises* of Saint Ignatius, it is not presented as a scholarly analysis of Saint Ignatius' life or spirituality. Hopefully, this book will be an invitation to, but not a replacement for, doing the *Spiritual Exercises*.

There are numerous authors of spiritual poetic verse in this publication. Picking one author out of the pack almost seems unfair. Yet, one author is a personal favorite. Teilhard de Chardin's S.J. words and life had a profound impact on me in college.

Forty years later, his poem on Hope still seems profound:

The day will come, after harnessing space, the

winds, the tides, and gravitation,

That we shall harness for God the Energies of Love.

And on that day, for the second time in the history of the world,

We shall have discovered FIRE...

Appreciate the *Exercises*. They will most probably set your heart on fire and help fill many other hearts with a feeling of gratitude. Accept this invitation. The *Exercises* do transform. You do not have to be a saint before you start them. Ignatius of Loyola is a great model for a spiritual journey because he was not "saintly" when he started the *Exercises*. When you finish the exercises, you will not be concerned about being good enough. It is not about being perfect or imperfect. It is not about being saint or sinner. It is about accepting that we are all a little "rascally", and all of us are made in the image and likeness of God. We are all good enough. We can take care of one another and achieve a personal relationship with God.

David O'Brien

Ignatian Associate

✝
Week One Of The Spiritual Exercises By Larry Gillick S.J.

· ·

The first week of the *Spiritual Exercises* calls the person to reflect upon God's love in creating everything. Then each person confronts that she or he also has been created personally as a gift. Then there comes the praying with the gifts of creation and how they are to be received and reverently used. Throughout the first week, there rides the *big question:* For what purpose am I, are we, created?

The rest of the first week offers the invitation to experience the loving response of God to us, even in our lack of reverently and gratefully responding to God's gifts. The first week does involve personally reflecting on our disorderly conduct, aka sin. The week is not so much about sin as it is about how this loving God does not give up on bringing us to our creational status as God's beloved family. The *Exercises* confront us with the conflict between what we say about who we are, because of our sin, and who God says we are, because of who God is.

Week One: God's Gifts To Us & Our Responding

··

Favorite Readings & Journal Notes

Genesis 2: 4-25

The Second Story of Creation:

This is the story of the heavens and the earth at their creation. When the LORD God made the earth and the heavens, there was no field shrub on earth and no grass of the field had sprouted, for the LORD God had sent no rain upon the earth and there was no man to till the ground, but a stream was welling up out of the earth and watering all the surface of the ground, then the LORD God formed the man out of the dust of the ground and blew into his nostrils the breath of life, and the man became a living being.

The LORD God planted a garden in Eden, in the east, and placed there the man whom he had formed. Out of the ground the LORD God made grow every tree that was delightful to look at and good for food, with the tree of life in the middle of the garden and the tree of the knowledge of good and evil.

A river rises in Eden to water the garden; beyond there it divides and becomes four branches. The name of the first is the Pishon; it is the one that winds through the whole land of Havilah, where there is gold. The gold of that land is good; bdellium and lapis lazuli are also there. The name of the second river is the Gihon; it is the one that winds all through the land of Cush. The name of the third river is the Tigris; it is the one that flows east of Asshur. The fourth river is the Euphrates.

Journal notes: On a daily basis, we can appreciate the God in creation by noting that the most distant galaxy sighted by the Hubble telescope is over 13 billion light years away. We have scanned the universe and life, as we know it, does not exist anywhere else.

The LORD God then took the man and settled him in the garden of Eden, to cultivate and care for it. The LORD God gave the man this order: You are free to eat from any of the trees of the garden except the tree of knowledge of good and evil. From that tree you shall not eat; when you eat from it you shall die.

The LORD God said: It is not good for the man to be alone. I will make a helper suited to him. So the LORD God formed out of the ground all the wild animals and all the birds of the air, and he brought them to the man to see what he would call them; whatever the man called each living creature was then its name. The man gave names to all the tame animals, all the birds of the air, and all the wild animals; but none proved to be a helper suited to the man.

So the LORD God cast a deep sleep on the man, and while he was asleep, he took out one of his ribs and closed up its place with flesh. The LORD God then built the rib that he had taken from the man into a woman. When he brought her to the man, the man said:

"This one, at last, is bone of my bones and flesh of my flesh; this one shall be called 'woman,' for out of man this one has been taken." That is why a man leaves his father and mother and clings to his wife, and the two of them become one body. The man and his wife were both naked, yet they felt no shame.

Genesis 3: 1-11
The Garden of Eden & Original Sin

Now the snake was the most cunning of all the wild animals that the LORD God had made. He asked the woman, "Did God really say, 'You shall not eat from any of the trees in the garden'? The woman answered the snake: "We may eat of the fruit of the trees in the garden; it is only about the fruit of the tree in the middle of the garden that God said, 'You shall not eat it or even touch it, or else you will die.'" But the snake said to the woman: "You certainly will not die! God knows well that when you eat of it your eyes will be opened and you will be like gods, who know good and evil." The woman saw that the tree was good for food and pleasing to the eyes, and the tree was desirable for gaining wisdom. So she took some of its fruit and ate it; and she also gave some to her husband, who was with her, and he ate it. Then the eyes of both of them were opened, and they knew that they were naked; so they sewed fig leaves together and made loincloths for themselves.

Journal notes: Ultimately, whatever we misuse will misuse us.

When they heard the sound of the LORD God walking about in the garden at the breezy time of the day, the man and his wife hid themselves from the LORD God among the trees of the garden. The LORD God then called to the man and asked him: Where are you? He answered, "I heard you in the garden; but I was afraid, because I was naked, so I hid." Then God asked: Who told you that you were naked? Have you eaten from the tree of which I had forbidden you to eat?

Ephesians 3: 14:19

For this reason I kneel before the Father, from whom every family in heaven and on earth is named, that he may grant you in accord with the riches of his glory to be strengthened with power through his Spirit in the inner self, and that Christ may dwell in your hearts through faith; that you, rooted and grounded in love, may have strength to comprehend with all the holy ones what is the breadth and length and height and depth, and to know the love of Christ that surpasses knowledge, so that you may be filled with all the fullness of God.

Journal notes: With the exception of God and my infinite desire to be infinitely loved, there is little, if anything, that is perfect.

Matthew 6: 9-15
The Lord's Prayer

"This is how you are to pray:

Our Father in heaven, hallowed be your name,

your kingdom come, your will be done,

on earth as in heaven.

Give us today our daily bread;

and forgive us our debts,

as we forgive our debtors;

and do not subject us to the final test,

but deliver us from the evil one.

If you forgive others their transgressions,

your heavenly Father will forgive you.

But if you do not forgive others,

neither will your Father forgive your transgressions.

Journal notes: We are our choices. Sometimes we choose to become more of what God is and sometimes we choose thinking we are the God.

Psalm 131: 1-3
Childlike Trust in the Lord. A Song of
Ascents, of David.

LORD, my heart is not proud;

nor are my eyes haughty.

I do not busy myself with great matters, with things too sublime for me.

Rather, I have stilled my soul,

Like a weaned child to its mother, weaned is my soul.

Israel, hope in the LORD, now and forever.

Journal notes: Teilhard de Chardin S.J. asked if we are human beings having a spiritual experience or spiritual beings having a human experience.

✝
Week One: God's Gifts To Us & Our Responding

Other Favorite Reading References

Genesis 1: 1-31

Genesis 12: 1-8

Psalm 51:

Psalm 91:

Psalm 103:

Psalm 105:

Psalm 106:

Psalm 139:

Revelation 21: 1-8

Colossians 1: 15-23

Matthew 7: 1-23

Matthew 13: 4-23

Week One: God's Gifts To Us & Our Responding Poetic Reflections

First Page
....

How shall we mold one another?

First impressions ...

Rhymes for all times!

Emotions that never cease!

A window to humble prayers

And humbler poetic reflection.

Less yours to peer inside

Than mine to see outside.

Come here often, I do not

Depends upon life's season.

Busy times, sadly many, pass by

Curtains drawn, forgot the reason.

Dark days, clouded by pain

Like thorns on my eyes,

Then prayers and forgiveness

Wash this window clean.

Better still, joyful days children, flowers and more

Fill me with Thanksgiving.

And so first page

Mold this with passion

For daily prayers and poetic reflections.

David O'Brien

First Principle

....

The goal

of our life is to be

with God forever.

We should not fix our desires

on health or sickness,

wealth or poverty, success or failure,

a long life or a short one.

For everything has the potential

of calling forth in us

a deeper response

to our life in God.

First Principle by St Ignatius

As paraphrased by David L Fleming S.J.

Masters and Pupils

When the pupil is ready, the master will appear.

Hindu Proverb

Love Affair

Love Affair

I have been invited

To enter into an intense love affair

With God.

Odd.

I feel so human

And wonder whether I am Worthy of God's attention And love.

I am content to know that

If God thought me unworthy, I would be set aside-- Ignored--

Cease to be— So I rest in

God's assessment of the Appropriateness of our relationship.

Do I approach God as sinner?

Or is it more appropriate to Come to God as "human"

"needy" "child"?

Probably not always as "sinner"--

Although it IS an appropriate label,

It tends to send me in a direction of Hiding from God—

When what I really want

Is to Stand in the open

And sing to the Creator of the Universe

"Here I Am" and

"I love You" and

"I hope You aren't too disappointed in me"

And receive God's humbling

"I love you, too" in return.

Martha Conway

Thoughts in Solitude

My Lord God, I have no idea where I am going.

I do not see the road ahead of me.

I cannot know for certain where it will end.

Nor do I really know myself, and the fact that I think

I am following your will does not mean that I am actually doing so.

But I believe that the desire to please you does in fact please you.

And I hope that I will never do anything apart from that desire.

And I know that, if I do this, you will lead me by the right road,

Though I may know nothing about it.

Therefore, I will trust you always though

I seem to be lost and in the shadow of death.

I will not fear, for you are ever with me,

And you will never leave me to face my perils alone.

Thomas Merton

Embrace It All

....

God speaks to each of us as he (she) makes us,

Then walks with us silently out of the night.

These are the words we dimly hear:

You, sent out beyond your recall, you're longing.

Embody me.

Flare up like flame and make big shadows I can move in.

Let everything happen to you, beauty and terror.

Just keep going. No feeling is final.

Don't let yourself lose me.

Nearby is the country they call life.

You will know it by its seriousness.

Give me your hand.

Rainer Maria Rilke

Conversion

....

O Beauty, so ancient and yet so new.

Too late have I known you, too late have I loved you.

I stand here in need of your mercy.

Rebuild me anew, fill my soul.

Let me seek, my soul thirsts for you.

You were always near me when I was far astray.

You stretched your hands out to me, but I turned away.

I reached out for creation not creator, the beauty created by your hand.

But even in the shadows, your love broke through.

You shouted out and broke through my deafness.

You burned brightly and chased away my blindness.

You breathed your fragrance upon me and even now do I yearn for you.

You touched me and I burn for your peace.

You have made me O God, to live forever in your love and

My heart will not rest until it rests in you.

Saint Augustine

Today and all it Offers

Mornings run together like a strand of pearls

An early rise, so serene, so full of hope.

Dawn peaks out with a cautious yawn.

Birds send a "Good Day" to neighboring flock.

Breezes chase the lingering clouds away.

Gone is the quiet that lives in the dark.

Rain has left "love drops" on leaves.

It is a table, set for seeing with the heart.

A special day it must be so.

The promise of endless wonder.

Today is everything we have.

A gift so precious, our arms are full.

Embrace us tenderly and take your leave.

Elizabeth Stemmer

Spiritual Exercises In Poetic Form

Lord my God,

When your love spilled over into creation,

You thought of me.

I am from love of love for love.

Let my heart, O God, always recognize, cherish,

and enjoy your goodness in all creation.

Direct all that is me toward your praise.

Teach me reverence for every person, all things.

Energize me in your service.

Lord, God

May nothing ever distract me from your love...

Neither health nor sickness

Wealth nor poverty

Honor nor dishonor

Long life nor short life.

May I never seek nor choose to be other than

You intend or wish.

Amen.

Jacqueline S. Bergan & Marie Schwan

Appreciation

Before I could say I am,

I was a spirit in the universe

Timelessly seeking the window

Framed into the house of man.

As with all who came before,

Or will journey in the future,

Love, conception and God's grace

Breathed life into my spirit.

Like Adam in the Garden of Eden,

I wrestle with my freedom.

To appreciate or take for granted

So many marvelous gifts.

I am in the time of my life.

Joyfully, everyday new wonders.

Sadly, everyday more partings.

Sadder still, time will not reverse.

A gift is never more precious

Than when I face its loss.

Such partings mark my life

And jolt me to new appreciation.

David O'Brien

Make Your Way To The Potter's House

I am the clay—

Slippery, unformed—

Trying to take a shape of my own choosing—

Other than the one You are trying to create.

I am too thick in some places-

Too fragile and thin in others—

Not a very good vessel ---yet.

You are the potter—

Patient, skillful and observant—sensitive to when the clay is

Out of balance—

Knowing what to do to

Thin out the thick spots

And strengthen the thin, weak areas—

Ready to re-do, to start over

Again and again.

I continue to try to be my own potter—

Trying to shape myself into my idea of

Your image of me—

And, each time, I slip out of my own hands

And crash to the ground—

I cannot seem to manage the potter's wheel

And be the clay at the same time.

So, I need to remember who is what—

I, the clay—

You, the potter.

And to trust that, no matter how many flaws there are,

You are, indeed, a patient potter—

Who will re-work me again and again—

And will never give up on me and move on

To other clay that might be more workable and beautiful.

I place all my trust in You, the persistent potter of my life.

Martha Conway

Daily Prayer
....

Help me to realize you in everyone I meet today.

Guide me as a Christian, father and friend.

Keep me alert to see and hear the truth.

Challenge me to be brave, honest and fair.

Give me patience, when I feel burdened.

Show me unconditional love, so I can forgive.

Let me be humble versus self-righteous and proud.

Enable me to let others see you in me.

And when this and all my days are done,

May I have done my best to do your will.

David O'Brien

Notes

. . . .

†

Week Two Of The Spiritual Exercises
By Larry Gillick S.J.

The second week is spent in going through the picture album of Christ's life. Ignatius invites the person praying through the *Exercises* to receive what Jesus is doing, not just for the person or persons of the stories, but more personally for the retreatant, as well. Ignatius asks the person to get into the picture and see, hear and smell what is going on, both in the Gospel narrative and in her or his own life. It is about Jesus' getting up close and personal and the retreatant doing the same.

Intimacy cannot be standardized. Each person meets Jesus according to how Jesus meets the person praying. God comes to us according to us. God's love adapts to and reverences each person uniquely. There is no measuring up; there are no expectations to be met. The retreatant is invited to show up and be open to what is being offered in each exercise involving the life of Jesus. We cannot love what we do not know. We cannot serve or follow what we do not love. In a simple sense, we hang out with the person of Jesus and begin interiorizing His style, His interior.

The second week invites the retreatant to get in contact with the question of *identity:Who are we and what are our values?* The Creator is trying to give us our identity and so, too, is the world around and within us. There is a struggle that has to be faced about to whom we belong. This struggle to answer this *big question* does result in some kind of a decision or *election* to follow Jesus more closely, according to the person's unique relationship with God.

Week Two: Call To Discipleship

Favorite Readings & Journal Notes

Luke 1:26-28
The Birth of Jesus Foretold

In the sixth month, the angel Gabriel was sent from God to a town of Galilee called Nazareth, to a virgin betrothed to a man named Joseph, of the house of David, and the virgin's name was Mary. And coming to her, he said, "Hail, favored one! The Lord is with you."

Luke 2: 41-52
The Boy Jesus in the Temple

Now every year his parents went to Jerusalem for the festival of the Passover. And when he was twelve years old, they went up as usual for the festival. When the festival was ended and they started to return, the boy Jesus stayed behind in Jerusalem, but his parents did not know it. Assuming that he was in the group of travelers, they went a day's journey. Then they started to look for him among their relatives and friends. When they did not find him, they returned to Jerusalem to search for him. After three days they found him in the temple, sitting among the teachers, listening to them and asking them questions. And all who heard him were amazed at his understanding and his answers. When his parents saw him they were astonished; and his mother said to him, "Child, why have you treated us like this? Look, your father and I have been searching for you in great anxiety."

He said to them, "Why were you searching for me? Did you not know that I must be in my Father's house?" But they did not understand what he said to them. Then he went down with them and came to Nazareth, and was obedient to them. His mother treasured all these things in her heart. And Jesus increased in wisdom and in years, and in divine and human favor.

> **Journal notes:** Be a disciple and not just a believer.

Matthew 4: 18-22
Jesus Calls the First Disciples

As he was walking by the Sea of Galilee, he saw two brothers, Simon who is called Peter, and his brother Andrew, casting a net into the sea; they were fishermen. He said to them, "Come after me, and I will make you fishers of men." At once they left their nets and followed him. He walked along from there and saw two other brothers, James, the son of Zebedee, and his brother John. They were in a boat, with their father Zebedee, mending their nets. He called them, and immediately they left their boat and their father and followed him.

Matthew 10: 1-14
The Mission of the Twelve

Then he summoned his twelve disciples and gave them authority over unclean spirits to drive them out and to cure every disease and every illness. The names of the twelve apostles are these: first, Simon called Peter, and his brother Andrew; James, the son of Zebedee, and his brother John; Philip and Bartholomew, Thomas and Matthew the tax collector; James, the son of Alphaeus, and Thaddeus; Simon the Cananean, and Judas Iscariot who betrayed him. Jesus sent out these twelve after instructing them thus, "Do not go into pagan territory or enter a Samaritan town. Go rather to the lost sheep of the house of Israel. As you go, make this proclamation: 'The kingdom of heaven is at hand.' Cure the sick, raise the dead, cleanse lepers, drive out demons. Without cost you have received; without cost you are to give. Do not take gold or silver or copper for your belts; no sack for the journey, or a second tunic, or sandals, or walking stick. The laborer deserves his keep. Whatever town or village you enter, look for a worthy person in it, and stay there until you leave. As you enter a house, wish it peace. If the house is worthy, let your peace come upon it; if not, let your peace return to you. Whoever will not receive you or listen to your words—go outside that house or town and shake the dust from your feet."

Journal notes: Christian leadership consists of spiritual guidance, being the light of Christ, motivating and providing direction in life. Being a leader in one's family, church, government or business is not about controlling, being in charge or expecting others to be submissive. To be a leader, we must represent and model what is good for others. We become true leaders after we have learned how to be a servant to God and those around us.

Luke 7: 36-47
A Sinful Woman Forgiven

A Pharisee invited him to dine with him, and he entered the Pharisee's house and reclined at table. Now there was a sinful woman in the city who learned that he was at table in the house of the Pharisee. Bringing an alabaster flask of ointment, she stood behind him at his feet weeping and began to bathe his feet with her tears. Then she wiped them with her hair, kissed them, and anointed them with the ointment. When the Pharisee who had invited him saw this he said to himself, "If this man were a prophet, he would know who and what sort of woman this is who is touching him, that she is a sinner." Jesus said to him in reply, "Simon, I have something to say to you." "Tell me, teacher," he said. "Two people were in debt to a certain creditor; one owed five hundred days wages and the other owed fifty. Since they were unable to repay the debt, he forgave it for both. Which of them will love him more?" Simon said in reply, "The one, I suppose, whose larger debt was forgiven." He said to him, "You have judged rightly." Then he turned to the woman and said to Simon, "Do you see this woman? When I entered your house, you did not give me water for my feet, but she has bathed them with her tears and wiped them with her hair. You did not give me a kiss, but she has not ceased kissing my feet since the time I entered. You did not anoint my head with oil, but she anointed my feet with ointment. So I tell you, her many sins have been forgiven; hence, she has shown great love. But the one to whom little is forgiven, loves little."

Matthew 5:1-20
The Sermon on the Mount; The Beatitudes

When he saw the crowds, he went up the mountain, and after he had sat down, his disciples came to him. He began to teach them, saying:

THE BEATITUDES

Blessed are the poor in spirit, for theirs is the kingdom of heaven.

Blessed are they who mourn, for they will be comforted.

Journal notes: They have been called the capital or deadly sins: pride, anger, covetousness, lust, gluttony, envy, and sloth. Since few, if any of us, can live a day without acting out some of these, we might have called them the daily sins.

Blessed are the meek, for they will inherit the land.

Blessed are they who hunger and thirst for righteousness, for they will be satisfied.

Blessed are the merciful, for they will be shown mercy.

Blessed are the clean of heart, for they will see God.

Blessed are the peacemakers, for they will be called children of God.

Blessed are they who are persecuted for the sake of righteousness, for theirs is the kingdom of heaven.

Blessed are you when they insult you and persecute you and utter every kind of evil against you because of me. Rejoice and be glad, for your reward will be great in heaven. Thus they persecuted the prophets who were before you.

The Similes of Salt and Light.

"You are the salt of the earth. But if salt loses its taste, with what can it be seasoned? It is no longer good for anything but to be thrown out and trampled underfoot. You are the light of the world. A city set on a mountain cannot be hidden. Nor do they light a lamp and then put it under a bushel basket; it is set on a lampstand, where it gives light to all in the house. Just so, your light must shine before others, that they may see your good deeds and glorify your heavenly Father.

Luke 15: 11-32
The Prodigal Son

Then Jesus said, "A man had two sons, and the younger son said to his father, 'Father, give me the share of your estate that should come to me.' So the father divided the property between them. After a few days, the younger son collected all his belongings and set off to a distant country where he squandered his inheritance on a life of dissipation. When he had freely spent everything, a severe famine struck that country, and he found himself in dire need. So he hired himself out to one of the local citizens who sent him to his farm to tend the swine.

Journal notes: We do not have to achieve anything to earn God's love. We merely have to allow ourselves to receive it.

And he longed to eat his fill of the pods on which the swine fed, but nobody gave him any. Coming to his senses he thought, 'How many of my father's hired workers have more than enough food to eat, but here am I, dying from hunger. I shall get up and go to my father and I shall say to him, "Father, I have sinned against heaven and against you. I no longer deserve to be called your son; treat me as you would treat one of your hired workers."' So he got up and went back to his father. While he was still a long way off, his father caught sight of him, and was filled with compassion. He ran to his son, embraced him and kissed him. His son said to him, 'Father, I have sinned against heaven and against you; I no longer deserve to be called your son.' But his father ordered his servants,

'Quickly bring the finest robe and put it on him; put a ring on his finger and sandals on his feet. Take the fattened calf and slaughter it. Then let us celebrate with a feast, because this son of mine was dead, and has come to life again; he was lost, and has been found.' Then the celebration began. Now the older son had been out in the field and, on his way back, as he neared the house, he heard the sound of music and dancing. He called one of the servants and asked what this might mean. The servant said to him, 'Your brother has returned and your father has slaughtered the fattened calf because he has him back safe and sound.' He became angry, and when he refused to enter the house, his father came out and pleaded with him. He said to his father in reply, 'Look, all these years I served you and not once did I disobey your orders; yet you never gave me even a young goat to feast on with my friends. But when your son returns who swallowed up your property with prostitutes, for him you slaughter the fattened calf.' He said to him, 'My son, you are here with me always; everything I have is yours. But now we must celebrate and rejoice, because your brother was dead and has come to life again; he was lost and has been found.'"

Journal notes: Asking for and giving forgiveness are powerful gifts, but they are just the beginning of the healing process. Although scorn, rejection and punishment from others are painful, the greatest punishments are those that we inflict upon ourselves. There is tremendous power in a person's smile, loving embrace or simple acceptance of one who has made a mistake. The ability to visualize another growing through the pain of a mistake can heal a person's shame and pave the way for them feeling God's love.

Week Two: Call To Discipleship

Other Favorite Reading References

Luke 1: 26-28

Luke 1: 39-56

Luke 2: 8-20

Luke 2:22-39

Luke 2: 51-52

John 2: 1-11

John 2: 13-22

John 11: 1-45

John 13: 1-30

Matthew 2: 19-25

Matthew 3: 13-17

Matthew 4: 18-22

Matthew 9:

Mark: 14: 44-54

Mark: 16: 1-11

Week Two: Call To Discipleship
Poetic Reflections

In the Kitchen
....

("In the sixth month the angel Gabriel…" Luke 1:26)

Bellini has it wrong.

I was not kneeling on my satin cushion

quietly at prayer, head slightly bent.

Painters always skew the scene,

as though my life were wrapped in silks,

in temple smells.

Actually I had just come back from the well,

placing the pitcher on the table,

I bumped against the edge,

spilling water on the floor.

As I bent to wipe it up,

there was a light against the kitchen wall

as though someone had opened

the door to the sun.

Rag in hand, hair across my face,

I turned to see who was entering, unannounced, unasked.

All I saw was light,

white against the timbers.

I heard a voice I had never heard.

I heard a greeting,

I was elected,

the Lord was with me,

I pushed back my hair,

stood afraid.

Someone closed the door.

And I dropped the rag.

Kilian McDonnell, OSB

Later That Night

I am still awake and it's very late.

What have I done?

What was I thinking?

Was that really a messenger from God?

Why do I impulsively say "yes"?

When thinking it over slowly might be wiser?

What will Joseph think?

What will my parents do?

What does it all mean—my son, savior of our people?

A ruler greater than David and wiser that Solomon?

What will be said about him?

Will I live in a palace—how could we make our savior

live in a poor village?

How will he get the right training/schooling?

Will he give me rich clothes and gold jewelry—so all the world

Will see how he cherishes his mother?

Will I have servants?

How could that be? We are poor!

And, besides, Joseph will not want to have anything to do with me

Now that I'm pregnant—and not by him.

Why would he believe my story of this night?

No one would believe such a tale.

Or will I have to flee with my child—

Cast out like Hagar—

Left to fend off dangers and try to protect myself and my child.

Will we be left alone?

How can I explain to my mother?

What will she say?

Will she send me away in disgrace?

Who will this child be?

King? Ruler? Freedom-fighter?

How big a kingdom is he to rule?

Will he know his destiny right from the beginning

—or will we have to discover it together?

Why would God entrust this to me?

I'm just a simple village girl.

Martha Conway

The Advent Season

It is not that I failed to see or appreciate the wonder of

Spring warmth on ice crystals and walks without winter coats, or

Summer baking rows of corn and naps under shaded trees, or

Fall apples baking in pies and deer in hay fields at dusk, or

Winter nights filled with stars and feet warmed against a fire.

It is my greater appreciation for the Advent Season

Seen in churches, hallways, and — yes — even stores

Expressed by family, friends, and strangers

I am in awe and forever challenged by the

Way our souls embrace the advent spirit of

Loving, forgiving, blessing and healing that comes from

Giving and preparing to receive Christ in our midst.

David O'Brien

Shoes of a Fisherman
....

To meet a whole man is an ennobling experience.

It cost so much to be a full man,

That there are very few who will have the enlightenment

Or the courage to pay the price.

One has to abandon altogether the search for security

And reach out to embrace the world like a lover,

And yet demand no easy return of love.

One has to accept pain as a condition of existence,

And has to court doubt and darkness as the cost of knowing.

One needs a will stubborn in conflict,

But apt always to the total acceptance

Of every consequence of living and dying

If a man is centered upon himself, even the smallest risk is too great for him

because both success and failure can destroy him. If he is centered upon God, then
no risk is too great, because success is already guaranteed.

The successful union of creator and creature,

Beside which everything else is meaningless.

(Coincidental Tribute to Teilhard de Chardin
in M.L. West's Fictional Work
"The Shoes of the Fisherman")

Alabaster Jar

I come into your presence As you sit in Simon's house.

The love and gentle acceptance That radiates from your eyes
Pulls me to you As magnetic north pulls the
Marker on a compass.

The alabaster jar I am holding No longer seems to be of value—
Breaking it open and Pouring the perfume on your head
Makes exquisite sense to me.

Your followers are angry with me— But you understand
My compelling need To lavish this perfume
on you—my gift to you.

You accept my gift—
And, in that acceptance,
Accept me—
Anchor my life in meaning.

Be my compass—
Lead me toward my life purpose
And continue to accept
My small acts of love.

Martha Conway

Thoughts From Egypt

The angry arm of Herod is long,

And can be felt even as far away as Egypt.

Joseph and I have found a place.

Our child is safe and I should be content

And grateful For being so well protected.

Why is it though,

That, even at this distance,

I am able to hear

The sounds of grief Sobbing

Wailing

Screaming

Coming all the way from Bethlehem?

How can it be that so many mothers

Are robbed of their sons—

So many babies destroyed—

In the frenzied attempt

To destroy my son?

I do not rest easy

Knowing the horrible price

Other mothers have had to pay.

Martha Conway

Memorable Men

....

When did they acquire their presence and blessing?

At birth, you could not tell nor did they even know.

Beyond the question of when is the question of what

differentiated them amongst so many fellows.

None were financially wealthy,

important titles they had not.

While generally fit of body,

their prime was in the past.

It was their presence that made the difference.

They listened and shared;

they valued moments with you.

Robert Carlisle earned his keep as a night watch man

and shared his avocation of carpentry by day.

It was not only the lesson of holding a hammer or saw,

but simply being there blessed with grandfather time.

Carlos Baressi labored in a factory installing windows in cars,

until he had a heart attack that could have broken his spirit.

Instead he asked with great care,"How are you doing young man?"

He listened and questioned intently.

In a moment, you knew you mattered.

Elliot Thoreson was a teacher for a college in North Dakota.

His naturally inquiring mind asked what you thought and felt.

At family or social gatherings he created and shared traditions

Remembered by all for his blessing of life and you.

Their gifts were not acquired in any particular moment;

for it was how they approached a lifetime of moments with you.

All are dead now.

Gone are their moments,

but their memories will live forever.

David O'Brien

Teach Me To Listen

Teach me to listen, O God

To those nearest me, my family, my friends, my co-workers.

Help me to be aware that no matter what words I hear,

the message, "Accept the person I am. Listen to me".

Teach me to listen, my caring God, to those far from me

The whisper of the hopeless,

The plea of the forgotten,

The cry of the anguished.

Teach me to listen, O God my mother, to myself.

Help me to be less afraid

To trust the voice inside

In the deepest part of me.

Teach me to listen, Holy Spirit, for your voice

In busyness and in boredom

In certainty and in doubt,

In noise and in silence.

Teach me, Lord, to listen. Amen.

John Veltri S.J.

Prayer For Humility

Let me have too deep a sense of humor ever to be proud.

Let me know my absurdity before I act absurdly.

Let me realize that when I am humble,

I am most human, most trustful,

And most worthy of your serious consideration.

Daniel A Lord, S.J.

Patient Trust

....

Above all, trust in the slow work of God.

We are quite naturally impatient in everything

to reach the end without delay.

We should like to skip the intermediate stages.

We are impatient of being on the way to

something unknown, something new.

And yet, it is the law of all progress

That it is made by passing through some stages of instability

And that it may take a very long time.

And so I think it is with you.

Your ideas mature gradually — let them grow,

Let them shape themselves, without undue haste.

Don't try to force them on, as though you could be today what time

(that is to say grace and circumstances acting on your own good will)

— will make of you tomorrow.

Only God could say what this new spirit

Gradually forming within you will be.

Give our Lord the benefit of believing

That his hand is leading you,

And accept the anxiety of feeling yourself

in suspense and incomplete.

Pierre Teilhard de Chardin S.J.

Notes

· · · · · · · · · ·

✝
Week Three Of The Spiritual Exercises
By Larry Gillick S.J.

The third week centers our attention intellectually and our hearts emotionally on the openness of Jesus to whom He was as a "Suffering Servant." The retreatant walks with, talks with Jesus as He experiences ultimate rejection even by His closest friends. We watch Him live His life gratefully even to the point of His physical death. We listen to His conversations with the Roman officials and with His disciples at His Last Supper. We listen to His words from the cross and stand with His mother and good friend at the foot of the cross.

We are invited to consider that if we decide to follow Him more closely, then we, too, will have to confront our own self-centered desires for the easy life, the successful life, the powerful life. Jesus died because He confronted the powerful and the pretentious. Those following Jesus will also be invited to a similar life and perhaps death.

There is a tendency during the considerations of His dying to be sad and guilty. There is some of that, of course, but ultimately our praying this week's *Exercises* results in a deep sense of being so loved by a God who did all this for the love of us all. The invitation again is for the retreatant to desire to follow that love no matter what the cost.

Week Three: Passion Of Christ

....

Favorite Readings & Journal Notes

Luke 22: 47-53
The Betrayal and Arrest of Jesus

While he was still speaking, a crowd approached and in front was one of the Twelve, a man named Judas. He went up to Jesus to kiss him. Jesus said to him, "Judas, are you betraying the Son of Man with a kiss?" His disciples realized what was about to happen, and they asked, "Lord, shall we strike with a sword?" And one of them struck the high priest's servant and cut off his right ear. But Jesus said in reply, "Stop, no more of this!" Then he touched the servant's ear and healed him. And Jesus said to the chief priests and temple guards and elders who had come for him, "Have you come out as against a robber, with swords and clubs? Day after day I was with you in the temple area, and you did not seize me; but this is your hour, the time for the power of darkness."

Luke 22: 54-62
Peter Denies Jesus

After arresting him they led him away and took him into the house of the high priest; Peter was following at a distance. They lit a fire in the middle of the court-yard and sat around it, and Peter sat down with them. When a maid saw him seated in the light, she looked intently at him and said, "This man too was with him." But he denied it saying, "Woman, I do not know him." A short while later someone else saw him and said, "You too are one of them"; but Peter answered, "My friend, I am not." About an hour later, still another insisted, "Assuredly, this man too was with him, for he also is a Galilean." But Peter said, "My friend, I do not know what you are talking about." Just as he was saying this, the cock crowed, and the Lord turned and looked at Peter; and Peter remembered the word of the Lord, how he had said to him, "Before the cock crows today, you will deny me three times."

> **Journal Notes**: God created us in the Garden of Eden. We rejected God's will in the Garden of Eden. Jesus chooses to follow God's will in a Garden of Gethsemane. God and the garden are still here and so is our choosing.

Mark 15: 5-19
Pilate Hands Jesus over to Be Crucified

Jesus gave him no further answer, so that Pilate was amazed. Now on the occasion of the feast he used to release to them one prisoner whom they requested. A man called Barabbas was then in prison along with the rebels who had committed murder in a rebellion. The crowd came forward and began to ask him to do for them as he was accustomed. Pilate answered, "Do you want me to release to you the king of the Jews?" For he knew that it was out of envy that the chief priests had handed him over. But the chief priests stirred up the crowd to have him release Barabbas for them instead. Pilate again said to them in reply, "Then what [do you want] me to do with [the man you call] the king of the Jews?" They shouted again, "Crucify him." Pilate said to them, "Why? What evil has he done?" They only shouted the louder, "Crucify him." So Pilate, wishing to satisfy the crowd, released Barabbas to them and, after he had Jesus scourged, handed him over to be crucified.

Mark 15: 16-20
The Soldiers Mock Jesus

The soldiers led him away inside the palace, that is, the praetorian, and assembled the whole cohort. They clothed him in purple and, weaving a crown of thorns, placed it on him. They began to salute him with, "Hail, King of the Jews!" and kept striking his head with a reed and spitting upon him. They knelt before him in homage. And when they had mocked him, they stripped him of the purple cloak, dressed him in his own clothes, and led him out to crucify him.

Luke 23:33-49
The Crucifixion

When they came to the place called the Skull, they crucified him and the criminals there, one on his right, the other on his left. Then Jesus said, "Father, forgive them, they know not what they do." They divided his garments by casting lots. The people stood by and watched; the rulers, meanwhile, sneered at him and said, "He saved others, let him save himself if he is the chosen one, the Messiah

Journal notes: Forgiveness is not easy, but it is for the giving. Forgiveness requires time, prayer for both parties, a belief in tomorrow's opportunities, and desire to let go of but not forget the hurt. If we were never hurt, we could not learn forgiveness.

of God." Even the soldiers jeered at him. As they approached to offer him wine they called out, "If you are King of the Jews, save yourself." Above him there was an inscription that read, "This is the King of the Jews." Now one of the criminals hanging there reviled Jesus, saying, "Are you not the Messiah? Save yourself and us." The other, however, rebuking him, said in reply, "Have you no fear of God, for you are subject to the same condemnation? And indeed, we have been condemned justly, for the sentence we received corresponds to our crimes, but this man has done nothing criminal." Then he said, "Jesus, remember me when you come into your kingdom." He replied to him, "Amen, I say to you, today you will be with me in Paradise."

The Death of Jesus.

It was now about noon and darkness came over the whole land until three in the afternoon because of an eclipse of the sun. Then the veil of the temple was torn down the middle. Jesus cried out in a loud voice, "Father, into your hands I commend my spirit"; and when he had said this he breathed his last. The centurion who witnessed what had happened glorified God and said, "This man was innocent beyond doubt." When all the people who had gathered for this spectacle saw what had happened, they returned home beating their breasts; but all his acquaintances stood at a distance, including the women who had followed him from Galilee and saw these events.

Matthew 28:11-15
Administering Evil

While they were going, some of the guards went into the city and told the chief priests all that had happened. They assembled with the elders and took counsel; then they gave a large sum of money to the soldiers, telling them, "You are to say, 'His disciples came by night and stole him while we were asleep.' And if this gets to the ears of the governor, we will satisfy him and keep you out of trouble." The soldiers took the money and did as they were instructed. And this story has circulated among the Jews to the present day.

Journal notes: Jesus's physical suffering was second only to the non-physical agony he experienced. Those he came to save murdered him. His friends deserted and denied him. For a moment, in humble human fashion, even he felt God had forsaken him.

Luke 4:18-19
Healing

"The Spirit of the Lord is upon me, because he has anointed me to bring good tidings to the poor. He has sent me to proclaim liberty to the captives and recovery of sight to the blind, to let the oppressed go free, to proclaim the year of the Lord's favor."

Journal Notes: Forgiveness is probably the most powerful gift we have. We cannot demonstrate meaningful love if we cannot forgive. What legacy would Christ have left behind had he responded to his attackers with anger and defensiveness? All of us make countless mistakes that require forgiveness. Granting forgiveness provides us with the ability to undo these mistakes, go on and learn from them. Likewise, anger and un-forgiveness arrest people in their mistakes and keep them "held bound" for extended periods of time. To be a forgiver, we must start by being humble and asking for forgiveness from God and those around us. While saying, "I forgive you," is a powerful statement, saying, "I'm sorry," is even more powerful.

Week Three: Passion Of Christ
Other Favorite Reading References

Matthew 18: 21-22

Matthew 26: 20-58

Matthew 27:

Romans 8: 35-39

Luke 19: 47-48

Luke 22:

Luke 23:

Mark 14:

Mark 15:

John 19: 13-27

Week Three: Passion Of Christ
Poetic Reflections

I Have Been Entombed

I have been entombed within the ego of self;

I have been dead within the walls of winter

I have long laid aside the hope I once knew;

Many forgotten truths Line the path of wilderness.

I have grown weary with the waiting cocoon;

I have sensed with sorrow the pain of transformation.

Yet, in graceful stillness of this early April morning,

I am greeted in love with inside Eastering.

I stand before this moment with silent rising sun

And page full of Scripture and I proclaim: I am coming forth!

I've left the linens of winter Lying there behind me;

I've shook off the dust of dead and I'm bounding forth in Spirit.

It is time to break loose. It is time to come forth.

It is time to allow life to wing its way into depths.

This is the season of my Savior,

The One whom God raised from the dead.

This is the moment of resurrection

And I know it is the right time.

For I am coming forth, coming forth from the tomb-

And just like God risen,

I feel bonded with the world,

I feel all brokenness brought unto one.

I'm on my way to bless bread with each of my dear friends;

I'm on my way to offer presence

to all those I meet on the road;

I'm on my way to bring resurrection

To all who need God's healing Life.

It is Easter and I proclaim:

I've been raised form the dead !

I am coming forth from the tomb !

Joyce Rupp

What I Asked For

....

I asked God for strength, that I might achieve,

I was made weak, that I might learn humbly to obey.

I asked for health, that I might do great things,

I was given infirmity, that I might do better things.

I asked for riches, that I might be happy,

I was given poverty, that I might be wise.

I asked for power, that I might have the praise of men,

I was given weakness, that I might feel the need of God.

I asked for all things, that I might enjoy life,

I was given life, that I might enjoy all things.

I got nothing that I asked for, but everything I had hoped for.

Almost despite myself, my unspoken prayers were answered.

I am, among all men, most richly blessed.

Prayer Attributed to a Civil War Soldier

Thursday Night

Jesus sits

Torn

Beaten

Exhausted

Waiting

No more to be done—

Just to see it through

Ready

Not wanting to be alone

He asks only one thing

In response to my

"What can I do"?

"Sit with me".

Martha Conway

Jesus Meets The Women Of Jerusalem

Wail with sadness—aware of their loss.

In a society where women are necessary-

But unimportant—

Wail with sadness—aware of their loss.

In a society where women are necessary-

But unimportant—

Unlike other men,

Jesus saw us

As important—

More importantly,

He saw us as we are. . .

Gifted

Limited

Petty

Loving

Generous

Human

Unlike other men,

He saw us as

Whole,

And valuable,

Children of God.

How can we ever be the same?

How can we bear to live in a world

Marked by His absence?

He gave our lives meaning—

Where will we find meaning

After He is gone?

Martha Conway

Veronica, Here I Stand

Unable to speak

Unable to carry Your burden

All that is left for me

Is to wipe Your face

They say the image of Your face

Is imprinted on the cloth

I say the image of Your face

Is imprinted on my heart.

Martha Conway

Mary's Arms

At birth

Wrapped in cloths placed in your arms.

Visited by shepherds and magi

Precious infant hope of the future.

At death

Removed from the cross placed in your arms

No one to visit body broken and battered

Precious man savior of the world.

Did you weep, Mary? Or did you walk?

In sorrowful, heart-shattering silence?

Knowing that your son must do what he came to do—

But at what terrible price

To you?

Martha Conway

September 11, 2001

....

Oh God where are you?

Forsaken, angry & confused

Newscasters, endless recording

Burning, screaming and falling.

Darkness to brightest day

Evil beyond nightmares

Hope suspended in fire

Melting America's steel.

In stairways orderly, crying

Firemen climbing, dying

Policeman searching, suffocating

Masses in churches, praying.

My brother by marriage

More hijacker's carnage

Flight 93 no greater love

Than to lay down one's life.

Deena's phone searching

Towers and skies for Tom.

Connection severed by batteries

Heroic union with God.

In memorials, benefits & rescues

In calls, hugs, and newer friendships

In prayers, kindness and humility

In dust, Oh God, there you are.

David O'Brien

What Am I To Do With Jesus?

"What am I to do with Jesus", Pilate asks the crowd.

Crucify him!

"What crime has he committed"?

Crucify him!

He has made us uneasy—

He upsets us—

He challenges us to a new way—

He confuses us—

He's different—

He doesn't live like we do—

Or talk like we do—

Follow our old rules as we have followed them—

Kill him!!

He makes us uncomfortable—

And we want to go back to our old ways.

Martha Conway

New Seeds of Contemplation

... So, instead of loving what you think is peace

Love others and love God above all

And, instead of hating the people you think are war mongers

Hate the appetite and the disorder in your own soul which are the causes of war.

If you love peace, then hate injustice, hate tyranny, hate greed...

But hate these things in yourself, not in another.

Thomas Merton

Perseverance In Trial

Consider it all joy, my brothers,

when you encounter various trials.

For you know that the testing of your faith

produces perseverance.

And let perseverance be perfect,

so that you may be perfect and complete,

lacking in nothing.

James 1

New Testament

Spiritual Father

Greatest gift ... birth of children

Dramatic changes ... for the better

Awakening, growing, loving, challenging

Still, the greatest of moments.

Hardest moments... children stumbling

Tragedies unfolding. Hopes and dreams crashing

Expectations building walls

Confrontations threatening relationships.

Greatest gifts, I'm sorrowful

My role and pain uncertain

Discipline and love, I've tried

I cry for solutions.

Oh, heavenly father help me

To be as compassionate as you

To be one with my children

Call forth my spiritual fatherhood.

Help me to teach, so they can gain self-knowledge

Help me to forgive, so they grow in love

Help me to accept, so they feel unconditional blessing

Holy father, hear my prayer.

David O'Brien

Betrayal

....

When I look at the pain

And injustice in the world—

And then look at the

Pain and betrayal in my experience of life,

I am filled with anger and resentment;

And I rail against the unfairness of it all.

I am filled with indignation—

And believe that I am

Entitled to be self-righteous.

And, perhaps, I am...

Except that

My heart,

Filled to the brim with judgments

Has no space left for you, Jesus.

How difficult it is

To ask that you

Break open my heart—

Toss the anger and resentment,

The indignation

And the judgments

To the winds—

So that my heart—

Broken—

But now empty

Can be filled with you;

And I can live as you

Would have me be.

Break me open—

Heal me—

Fill me—

I am yours.

Martha Conway

Grace and Tribulation

Our Lord and Savior lifted up his voice

And Said with incomparable majesty

Let all men know that grace comes after tribulation.

Let them know that, without the burden of affliction,

It is impossible to reach the heights of grace.

Let them know that the gifts of grace increase as the struggles increase.

Let men take care not to stray and be deceived.

This is the only true stairway to Paradise, and without the cross

They can find no road to climb to heaven.

Saint Rose of Lima

Notes

· · · · · · · · · ·

✝

Week Four Of The Spiritual Exercises By Larry Gillick S.J.

The fourth week is spent in praying with the events of Christ's Resurrection. He rises to raise the minds and spirits of His dispersed followers. He goes about collecting and reuniting the disappointed and discouraged. His death was not an ending, but a continuation. We watch Jesus offer peace, reconciliation and a sense of mission to His little group. We use the powers of imagination again to watch Him meet His mother, who had stayed faithfully watching at the cross. There is a sense of joy and meaningfulness to our staying faithful to our own decisions and crosses.

The retreatant is invited to consider the cost of discipleship. We are invited through the contemplations of this week to consider the investments we are being called to make and our subsequent sacrifices. The Cross will lead to the Crown, but each person has to consider the cost. Some of His friends want to take the "Jerusalem bypass" and live the *la-la* life of avoidance and noninvolvement. Jesus rose from the dead to bring us all to life. He was faithful to who He was. Watching Him during this week of the *Exercises* moves us to embrace our infidelities. Like the fleeing and denying friends of the third week, we continually find ourselves being found, blest and sent to continue His Resurrection in our lives and others' lives.

Week Four: Resurrection

Favorite Readings

Psalm 150: 1-6

Hallelujah!

> Praise God in his holy sanctuary; give praise in the mighty dome of heaven.
>
> Give praise for his mighty deeds; praise him for his great majesty.
>
> Give praise with blasts upon the horn, praise him with harp and lyre.
>
> Give praise with tambourines and dance, praise him with strings and pipes.
>
> Give praise with crashing cymbals, praise him with sounding cymbals.
>
> Let everything that has breath give praise to the LORD!
>
> Hallelujah!

John 14-25-26

"I have told you this while I am with you. The Advocate, the Holy Spirit that the Father will send in my name, he will teach you everything and remind you of all that I told you.

Luke 24:30:53

And it happened that, while he was with them at table, he took bread, said the blessing, broke it, and gave it to them. With that their eyes were opened and they recognized him, but he vanished from their sight. Then they said to each other, "Were not our hearts burning within us while he spoke to us on the way and opened the scriptures to us?" So they set out at once and returned to

---

Journal notes: Our being created in the image and likeness of God was not an accident. God is with us as much today as God was in the Garden of Eden. Creation is still unfolding.

Jerusalem where they found gathered together the eleven and those with them who were saying, "The Lord has truly been raised and has appeared to Simon!" Then the two recounted what had taken place on the way and how he was made known to them in the breaking of the bread.

Jesus Appears to His Disciples

While they were still speaking about this, he stood in their midst and said to them, "Peace be with you." But they were startled and terrified and thought that they were seeing a ghost. Then he said to them, "Why are you troubled? And why do questions arise in your hearts? Look at my hands and my feet, that it is I myself. Touch me and see, because a ghost does not have flesh and bones as you can see I have." And as he said this, he showed them his hands and his feet.

While they were still incredulous for joy and were amazed, he asked them, "Have you anything here to eat?" They gave him a piece of baked fish; he took it and ate it in front of them. He said to them, "These are my words that I spoke to you while I was still with you, that everything written about me in the law of Moses and in the prophets and psalms must be fulfilled." Then he opened their minds to understand the scriptures. And he said to them, "Thus it is written that the Messiah would suffer and rise from the dead on the third day and that repentance, for the forgiveness of sins, would be preached in his name to all the nations, beginning from Jerusalem. You are witnesses of these things. And behold I am sending the promise of my Father upon you; but stay in the city until you are clothed with power from on high."

The Ascension of Jesus

Then he led them out as far as Bethany, raised his hands, and blessed them. As he blessed them he parted from them and was taken up to heaven. They did him homage and then returned to Jerusalem with great joy, and they were continually in the temple praising God.

> **Journal notes**: It is significant how many times Jesus greeted his disciples with, "Peace be with you." Everyday life presents us with opportunities to respond to situations with anger and rejection. A peacemaker must be more than loving, forgiving, and healing. As a "Peacemaker," we must do more than live peacefully. We must take the risks associated with truly initiating peace. If you wait for another person to initiate peace, you may lose the opportunity.

John 21:15-19

When they had finished breakfast, Jesus said to Simon Peter, "Simon, son of John, do you love me more than these?" He said to him, "Yes, Lord, you know that I love you." He said to him, "Feed my lambs." He then said to him a second time, "Simon, son of John, do you love me?" He said to him, "Yes, Lord, you know that I love you." He said to him, "Tend my sheep." He said to him the third time, "Simon, son of John, do you love me?" Peter was distressed that he had said to him a third time, "Do you love me?" and he said to him, "Lord, you know everything; you know that I love you." Jesus said to him, "Feed my sheep. Amen, amen, I say to you, when you were younger, you used to dress yourself and go where you wanted; but when you grow old, you will stretch out your hands, and someone else will dress you and lead you where you do not want to go." He said this signifying by what kind of death he would glorify God. And when he had said this, he said to him, "Follow me."

John 15:9-12
Love One Another

As the Father loves me, so I also love you. Remain in my love. If you keep my commandments, you will remain in my love, just as I have kept my Father's commandments and remain in his love. "I have told you this so that my joy may be in you and your joy may be complete. This is my commandment: love one another as I love you.

Philippians 2:1-8

Service to One Another
Everyday

If there is any encouragement in Christ, any solace in love, any participation in the Spirit, any compassion and mercy, complete my joy by being of the same mind, with the same love, united in heart, thinking one thing. Do nothing out of selfishness or out of vainglory; rather, humbly regard others as more important than yourselves, each looking out not for his own interests, but also everyone for those of others. Have among yourselves the same attitude that is also yours

---

Journal notes: Fill yourself and those around you with a sense of joy. Christ's life and resurrection spoke to the strength and wonder of ridding ourselves of fear, worry, and anxiety. "Be not afraid, I go before you," asks us to remember that if we believe and wait in joy, all will be well. Express your appreciation for these wonders to all that you meet and truly make a difference in life.

in Christ Jesus, Who, though he was in the form of God, did not regard equality with God something to be grasped. Rather, he emptied himself, taking the form of a slave, coming in human likeness; and found human in appearance, he humbled himself, becoming obedient to death, even death on a cross.

Journal notes: God is available to us every day. Imagine God in the room right now! While God asks us to be in service to one another, we are first and foremost asked to forgive and love each other. Loving those who love us back is easy. Be not afraid.

Week Four: Resurrection
....

Other Favorite Reading References

Mark: 16: 1-11

John 15: 1-9

John 20: 24-29

John 21: 1-17

Matthew 28:

Luke 24:

Acts: 1: 1-12

1 Corinthians 15:

Week Four: Resurrection
Poetic Reflections

This Is What It Means To Seek God Perfectly

....

To have a will that is always ready

To fold back within itself

And draw all the powers of the soul,

Down from its deepest center,

To rest in silent expectancy

For the coming of God.

Poised in tranquil and effortless concentration

Upon the point of my dependence on him,

To gather all that I am,

And have all that I can possibly suffer or do or be,

And abandon them all to God

In the resignation of a perfect love and blend forth

Pure trust in God to do his will.

Thomas Merton

New Seeds of Contemplation

Come and See

Come where?

Closer to me

Into my heart.

From what?

Your pain and

Your small view of life.

To what?

Joy and

Peace and

Closeness and

Quiet.

See what?

What will you show me?

Where will you take me?

What will you ask of me?

Who will I become?

Come and see.

Martha Conway

It's A Hard Life

....

It's a hard life, God—

To live in a world that needs salvation—

It's hard.

To live with Jesus—

--walking from town to town

--never staying in one place

--never knowing what he will say or do next

--not knowing what he means by those stories he tells

--but leaving family and job and walking with him—

It's hard.

To have supper with Jesus on Thursday--

--to have him say goodbye

--to let him wash our feet

--to have his going away gift be simple bread and wine

--to hear him saying strange things about body and blood and betrayal

--to try to stay awake with him in the garden—

It's hard.

To suffer with him on Friday—

--to watch him be tortured

--to listen to him being mocked

--to hear him denied

--to watch him carry his cross—and stumble

(our Jesus—stumbling?)

--to hear the sounds of crucifixion

--to watch him die

--to be unable to know what to say to his mother

It's hard.

To wait on Saturday—

--to feel empty and afraid

--to not know what to do or where to go

--to not understand why this happened

--to want to be with him but not knowing where he is

--to face having to return to the villages we came from with no Jesus to

give our life meaning

--to be lonely and scared and unfocused and hopeless

--to believe that this wonderful journey and mission is over—

It's hard.

To awaken on Sunday morning—

--to hear (from Mary, of all people) that the rock is rolled back

--to hear that the tomb is empty

--to hear that he is gone

--to see for ourselves the wrappings

--to be told, by a woman, that he is risen, but

--to be told, by men in authority, that the body had been stolen

--to not know what to believe

--to not know what it all means—

It's hard

To be alive, 2000 years later—

--believing

--wanting to walk with him

--trying to decide which Jesus to follow

the miracle worker?

the parable teller?

the Eucharist giver?

the sacrifice?

the entombed absent one?

the risen one?

Entombed, Jesus would be an easier Jesus to follow—

--I could be amazed at his miracles

--I could be amused and taught by his stories

--I could enjoy the Eucharist

--I could appreciate his sacrifice

--and I could believe that none of this really applies to me

because he is now in the tomb and it's over.

But, it's hard, God—very hard—

Because he is risen

And he expects me to live my life as if that is true for me—

He is once again here—present—walking with—and teaching

His followers.

He refuses to stay put

And continues to walk along, beckoning me to come too--

Asking me to live like a follower of a Risen Jesus—

Wanting me to become his friend

Expecting me to do his work and

Insisting that I be his message—

And that part is the hardest of all.

Martha Conway

An Aging

Armed with lectures and books

Written by other learned men,

I debated the existence of god.

My collegiate rite to determine.

Russell, Leary, Kant & Nietzsche,

So thorough was their reasoning,

I let them carry me

From one extreme to the other.

With King, Mandela, Camus & others,

I journeyed social justice.

So proud I had become,

My answers preceded questions.

Then children, mortgages and more

Drove me to forget the poor.

My accounts and worries grew.

No time for prayerful reflections.

Now the old debate

To believe in God or not,

Is so much easier

For God, I know, I'm not.

David O'Brien

Gratitude

....

Gratitude unlocks the fullness of life.

It turns what we have into enough, and more.

It turns denial into acceptance, chaos to order, confusion to clarity.

It can turn a meal into a feast, a house into a home, a stranger into a friend.

Gratitude makes sense of our past, brings peace for today,

and creates a vision for tomorrow.

Melody Beattie

Christmas Prayer 2001

Help us, Oh God

To go beyond Christmas celebrations,

Guide us to see what we have missed

And miss what we have seen.

In September's pain, we discovered You

And our need to love one another.

In Christmas we are reborn

With You in innocence and joy.

Empty chairs at holiday tables

Remind us that the evil of a few

Is not as powerful as the goodness of so many,

No greater love, than to lay down one's life.

In all our other relationships,

It is in giving that we receive.

Yet with You, we only need to accept

The gift You gave so long ago.

Keep us alert to see and hear the truth.

Show us your unconditional love,

So we can forgive others and ourselves

And realize You in everyone we meet

This Christmas season

Grant us the humility to accept Your gift,

The remembrance of Your love, all year long

Come Lord Jesus, hear our prayer.

David O'Brien

Unless
....

You can go to the tomb—but you won't find Jesus there.

Jesus will call you by name—but you cannot hold Him in the old way.

Jesus will appear—over and over again—

And you will not see Him—

You will not recognize Him—

You will not believe in Him—

Unless---Unless what?

Unless you turn away from the tomb

And turn to the work that God has given you to do—

Is it simple? Mundane? Not very exciting?

Do you need more drama?

The tomb will give you drama.

You can weep and sob and tear you hair

And be as dramatic as you want

But, when it's all over,

Jesus isn't there.

Unless you give up focusing only on Him,

And turn to the suffering in your cities—

Wash the feet of the homeless—

Touch gently the lonely elderly—

Hold with love an angry, grieving neighbor—

Listen grace-fully to a struggling lost teenager—

Treat an immigrant mother with utmost dignity and respect—

You will not see Him.

Is it simple? Mundane? Not very fun or exciting? Too bad!

You must give up your personal clutching of Jesus—

And turn with open hands and heart to those He loves.

Jesus walks among us every day

And we do not see Him

Hear Him, Answer Him, Love Him

Because we think He should be different than He is.

We look for Lord and Master—

When He is Neighbor and Brother.

We seek the Lord of the Universe and look for glory

When He is there, right in front of us—

Teaching us to be love.

Martha Conway

An Irish Blessing

I wish you not a path devoid of clouds,

Nor a life on a bed or roses.

Nor, that you might never need regret,

Nor that you should never feel pain.

No, this is not my wish for you. My wish for you is:

That you might be brave in times of trial

When other's lay crosses upon your shoulders.

When mountains must be climbed and chasms crossed,

When hope scarce shines through.

When every gift God gave you might grow along with you,

And let you give the gift of joy to all who care for you.

That you might always have a friend who is worth that name.

Whom you can trust.

And hope will be, in times of sadness,

Who will defy the storms of life by your side.

One more wish for you:

That in every hour of joy and pain, you may be close to God.

This is my wish for you and those who are close to you.

This is my hope for you, now and forever.

Irish Folklore

108

Praying

It doesn't have to be

the blue iris, it could be

weeds in a vacant lot, or a few

small stones; just

pay attention, then patch

a few words together and don't try

to make them elaborate, this isn't

a contest but the doorway

into thanks, and a silence in which

another voice may speak.

Mary Oliver

Waiting

....

Early on, I sought my own identity.

A man whose definition needed time and grace.

I searched for many things in different places over time.

As journey's stages advanced my created self emerged.

But created self asked for more than its own nurturing.

Without knowing why I asked for soul mate,

Someone who appreciated life

And gently embraced creation,

Strong character and gentle touch

A beautiful mate in and out.

Waiting focused the image of my definition and yours.

I knew you when I saw you walk across the floor.

Now we get to appreciate life's waiting and becoming.

Joining hands and visions

Soul mates you and I.

David O'Brien

Fall In Love

....

Nothing is more practical than finding God,

That is, than falling in love in a quite absolute, final way

What you are in love with,

What seizes your imagination,

Will affect everything.

It will decide what will get you out of bed in the morning,

What you do with your evenings,

How you spend your weekends,

What you read

What you know,

What breaks your heart, and what amazes you with joy and gratitude.

Fall in love,

Stay in love,

And it will decide everything

Fall in love with Christ; it will change everything.

Pedro Arrupe

Superior General

Society of Jesus

Notes

. . . .

✝
The Final Week By Larry Gillick S.J.
....

The final prayer exercise is a consideration again of all the gifts with which this loving God continues to bless us. As with Ignatius, who came down from his mountain retreat, the modern maker of the *Exercises* will be moved to do something. The retreatant offers his or her mind, memory and entire will to the Divine Giver and trusts that only God's love and grace are necessary, and will be riches enough.

As with physical exercise, when we stop and start again, we experience the muscles saying, "Don't ever stop again; it is too painful." One who begins the *Spiritual Exercises* is so influenced that he or she never stops making them. The Exercises are not a program or workshop, but a way of receiving life and living more freely what has been given to us. One does not actually make the *Spiritual Exercises*; rather, the *Exercises* make the person a fuller receiver of her or his creation. Ignatian Spirituality flows from these *Exercises* into the personal lives and missions of those who do come face to face with Jesus and themselves.

Ignatian Associates

Ignatian Associates are Catholic adults, married and single. The community founding was inspired in 1991 during the Ignatian Year – which celebrated the 450th Anniversary of the existence of the Society of Jesus and the 500th Anniversary of the birth of St. Ignatius of Loyola, and encouraged by the Document on "Cooperation With the Laity in Mission" from the 34th General Congregation of the Society of Jesus. Begun in 1992, the Ignatian Associates are an innovative extension of the 450 year Jesuit tradition of service to our Church and world.

Formation is rooted in the Spiritual Exercises of St. Ignatius. Following a two-year formation program, Ignatian Associates may accept an invitation to make public "Promises" of Simplicity of Life, Fidelity to the Gospel and to our Associate and Jesuit Companions, and Apostolic Availability. Currently, there are three communities of Ignatian Associates within the Wisconsin Province of the Society of Jesus. These are located in Milwaukee, Wisconsin, Omaha, Nebraska, and the Twin Cities of Minneapolis and St. Paul in Minnesota. Ignatian Associates serve in schools, universities, health care, social service programs, parishes, and a variety of business and other settings. Some work in traditional Jesuit institutions and ministries, while others bring the mission of Christ and the Jesuits to new situations. The Associates learn to stretch their abilities to minister in different cultural contexts and walk with the marginalized and poor.

Apostolic Life

Ignatian Associates are apostolic in that they work toward building the Reign of God. Desiring to enrich who they are as "called and sent people," Apostolic Availability is promised. Centered in Ignatian Spirituality, Associates strive to live a faith that gives witness to Christ's Word and work in the world, a faith that evangelizes culture, promotes justice, and exercises a preferential love for the poor and outcast in our society and throughout the world.

First and foremost, Ignatian Associates strengthen and deepen holy and existing commitments regarding baptism, marriage, family, community, and work. This also encompasses parenting children and developing our families to see God in all things while respecting each and every human being as a gift of God.

In addition, the Associates are committed to individual and community apostolic projects that promote the Reign of God in the universal mission shared with the Society of Jesus, and indeed, with the entire Church. Time, talent, treasure, and prayerful discernment about human needs and how these might be addressed determine how individual and communal projects are shaped.

Community apostolic projects bring members together in a special way through a common focus on apostolic work in prayer. Though active participation in individual Associate communities varies according to the circumstances of a project and makeup of a specific community, all Associate members prayerfully support their communal projects.

Formation

The purpose of formation is to draw us into the life of Christ and bring us true freedom to serve others. Each Ignatian Associate commits to this lifelong growth process.

Initial formation is a two year process. It includes the Retreat in Daily Life and a study of the history, mission, and philosophy of the Jesuits and the Ignatian Associates. Formation deepens prayer, faith sharing, and reflection on apostolic activity as well as developing group intimacy and trust. In addition, formation emphasizes the Catholic Church's teachings on social justice and the call to lay leadership and service. The study and discernment of the Promises of Simplicity of Life, Fidelity, and Apostolic Availability are integral. Hands-on apostolic experiences and prayerful reflection on the same are critical to Ignatian Associate formation.

Formators are "Promised" Associates and Jesuits who have a background in Ignatian Spirituality/theology and interpersonal and group dynamics. They serve as companions/mentors to Associates in formation.

Local communities will provide Promised Associates with ongoing formation opportunities including, but not limited to, retreats and theological reflection on apostolic activities and the Spiritual Exercises.

For additional information about the Ignatian Associates please access

http://www.ignatianassociates.org/

Author Acknowledgements

Martha Conway, Ignatian Associate, for "Love Affair", "Make Your Way to the Potter's House", "Later That Night", "Alabaster Jar", "Thoughts from Egypt", "Thursday Night", "Veronica, Here I Stand", "Mary's Arms", "Jesus Meets the Women of Jerusalem", "What Am I to do With Jesus", "Betrayal", "It's a Hard Life", "Unless", and "Come and See" reprinted with permission from Martha Conway.

Larry Gillick S.J. for the general weekly introductions to the Spiritual Exercises: Week One-God's Gifts To Us & Our Responding; Week Two-Call to Discipleship; Week Three-Passion of Christ; Week Four-Resurrection, and Week Five-Continuing Our Appreciation and Gratitude for God's Love and Grace reprinted with permission from Larry Gillick S.J.

Kilian McDonnell OSB, for "*In The Kitchen*" from the title, *Swift, Lord, You Are Not*, Copyright 2003 by Order of Saint Benedict. Published by Liturgical Press dba Saint John's University Press, Collegeville, Minnesota. Reprinted with permission.

Elizabeth Stemmer for "*Today and All It Offers*" reprinted with permission from Elizabeth Stemmer.

All scriptural quotations are taken from the "*New American Bible*". The reprinting is done in compliance with the rules of Confraternity of Christian Doctrine (CCD) which owns the copyright for the *New American Bible, revised edition* translation.

John Veltri S.J. for "*Teach Me to Listen*" reprinted with permission of Institute of Jesuit Resources © Saint Louis, MO. "*Teach Me to Listen*" was re-printed in "*Hearts on Fire*", edited by Michael Harter S.J. All rights reserved.

David Fleming S.J. for "*First Principle*" reprinted with permission of Institute of Jesuit Resources © Saint Louis, MO. "*First Principle*" was re-printed in "*Hearts on Fire*", edited by Michael Harter S.J. All rights reserved.